Praise for

The ThirdPath Leader: Reimagining Work, Love, and Leadership

"ThirdPath Institute and Jessica DeGroot have been leading the charge for a more sustainable—and less overwhelmed—approach to work and life for over 20 years." —Brigid Schulte, author of *Overwhelmed*

"The best solutions for sharing household responsibilities help each person own the responsibilities they have. The Guide will help you do just that." —Eve Rodsky, author of *Fair Play*

"At a time when the rules of work-life balance are—finally—being rewritten, Jessica DeGroot is a crucial voice. Her unique experience and in-depth understanding of the challenges faced by caregivers has led to a slew of successful programs and concrete changes inside businesses and other organizations. Everyone who cares about this issue and is committed to gender equality at work and home will benefit from her exceptional insight." —Josh Levs, author of *All In*

"A challenge to relationships is not from disagreements, but from destructive disagreements. The ThirdPath Leader provides couples with effective and dramatic new ways to rebalance work and family responsibilities. The result is an improved relationship that promotes better tools to resolve disagreements and enhance the experience of fairness, consideration and love between partners." —B. Hibbs, author of *Try to See it My Way: Being Fair in Love and Marriage*

"ThirdPath Institute has grown a community of leaders who have always helped their teams work more flexibly. Long before the pandemic, they promoted hybrid, virtual and flexible work as a strategy for engagement and fulfillment. The ThirdPath Leader captures their wisdom in a beautifully written and illustrated guide that will make it easy for anyone to build a work life they love." —Kyra Cavanaugh, author of *Who Works Where, [And Who Cares?]*

"An essential ingredient of a Whole-Person Workplace is having leaders who are role models of a healthy work and life balance and who do their part to avoid chronic overwork. Jessica DeGroot has been educating the world about these ideas since founding ThirdPath Institute. The case studies and exercises in the ThirdPath Leader will help you become that role r `` `` ``
—Scott Behson, author of *The Whole-Person W(*

D1665809

"Jessica DeGroot started ThirdPath to help parents redesign their work lives so that both partners could support the family financially and care for their children. Many families have learned from her how to redesign their work to reach this double goal. She then expanded the focus to help leaders support their teams to follow a "third path." The ThirdPath Leader is the culmination of all that they have learned, an excellent resource for leaders and for all people to help them think in new ways—both at work and home."
—Lotte Bailyn, author of, *Breaking the Mold: Redesigning Work for Productive and Satisfying Lives*

"So many men have a nagging sense they aren't the spouses and fathers they want to be. Jessica DeGroot gives men permission to find a better way."
—Ed Frauenheim, author of *Reinventing Masculinity*

"Parents who launch their "third path" journey while planning for parental leave quickly learn that by helping themselves, they are also helping their organizations." —Amy Beacom, author of *The Parental Leave Playbook*

Jessica DeGroot,
President and Founder
ThirdPath Institute

THE THIRDPATH LEADER

Reimagining Work, Love, and Leadership

ThirdPath Institute
P.O. Box 9275, Philadelphia, PA 19139
thirdpath.org

ThirdPath Institute is a 501(c)3 nonprofit that assists individuals, families and organizations in redesigning work and life to create time for family, community and other life priorities. We provide a road map for individuals and leaders to design an integrated approach so everyone can succeed at work while caring well for our loved ones and communities. Through this work, and in collaboration with others, we encourage more progressive conversations at home, support more flexible workplaces and push for improved public policy.

The ThirdPath Leader: Reimagining Work, Love, and Leadership
April 2022

First Edition, 2022

ISBN: 978-1-66785-598-1

Printed in the United States of America

Thank you, Whit Honea, for helping ThirdPath create this amazing guide. Whit Honea is the author of *The Parents' Phrase Book* (Simon & Schuster) and co-founder of the philanthropic organization Dads 4 Change. His writing can be found at Fandango, Disney, Today, *Good Housekeeping*, *Stand Magazine*, and *The Washington Post*. Deemed "the activist dad" by UpWorthy and one of the "funniest dads on Twitter" by Mashable, Whit has been nominated for a Pushcart Prize and is the 2015 winner of the Iris Award for Best Writing. He lives in the greater Los Angeles area with his wife, two sons, and lots of pets.

Contents

SECTION 1—IMAGINE AN INTEGRATED LIFE

SECTION 2—THE 5 BIGGEST BARRIERS

SECTION 3—THE ROADMAP

ThirdPath Leaders learn how to get on the same page and hold each other gently accountable as they reach for their professional and family goals.

ThirdPath Leaders develop a set of skills that helps them work smarter, ensuring there is always plenty of time for their most important work.

ThirdPath Leaders learn how to leave breathing room for what's most important, as well as time to plan for what's coming next.

ThirdPath Leaders discover working as a team at home helps them anticipate the changing needs of their families.

ThirdPath Leaders get clear about life priorities by becoming intentional around creating both time and financial buffers to better manage the future.

ThirdPath Leaders understand that the unexpected will happen. Teamwork helps them navigate each change—whether it's challenging or delightful.

SECTION 4—THE THIRDPATH LEADER

The skills first developed when integrating work and life become the skills ThirdPath Leaders draw from to better manage their teams.

Life outside of work is always in flux. Developing a ThirdPath Leader mindset will serve you now and for the rest of your life.

Our community can be a resource to help you plan your next step.

THE THIRDPATH LEADER:
REIMAGINING WORK, LOVE, AND LEADERSHIP

Before the pandemic, work and family probably felt like a teeter-totter, with paid work too often pressed down to the ground and caregiving demands crammed on top of a long workday.

Or maybe you wondered if you could even start a family, worried you wouldn't have time to be the parent you wanted to be, not to mention time for yourself or as a couple.

In professional careers, paid work is always going to take up all available time, every minute you don't assign elsewhere. Tradition, society, and work cultures that reward a work-first mindset all contribute to this problem. They are formidable and hard to budge, but at ThirdPath Institute, we know how to shift the weight as you see fit.

Part of the problem is that for too many professionals, we were trained to see this balancing act as a solo act, that stereotypical female with a baby in one hand and briefcase in the other. She's the only one who needed to balance things. Luckily, we've been fighting to change this stereotype by growing a vibrant community of people who see men and women as equally skilled at providing care for children and aging loved ones and equally capable of integrating work and family.

By working together—whether it's two moms, two dads, or mom and dad—these parents are writing a different kind of script, one that goes something like this: We are in this together. We're going to get smart about what we want from life so we can continue to succeed at work and have plenty of time for the things that we really care about. We will work together to better understand what it is we need and then work together to meet these goals.

Obviously, different families have different needs and goals. There isn't a one-size-fits-all solution. But after over two decades of research and advocacy, we've learned a thing or two about the different elements that parents need to explore so they can achieve their preferred approach to work and family alongside their professional goals.

We've learned, we've taught, and we've worked with an amazing community doing bold and exciting things. It has been, and continues to be, a highly successful undertaking. Let us share what we have learned. Let us help you discover your own unique "third path"—an integrated approach to work and life.

BECAUSE WE WANT TO

In a world where most people combine work with something else, people following a third path have shown us that we can do a better job of meeting our responsibilities at work when we have time for what matters outside of work.

This is what Michelle and Rob wanted, but when they were balancing the needs of work and the care of their first child, they noticed that the majority of successful parents in their line of work were either fathers whose wives didn't work outside the home or parents who had full-time nannies.

Michelle and Rob were observing the traditional and modern-day leadership paths:

- **The First Path:** One parent prioritizes work. The other prioritizes family.
- **The Second Path:** Both parents prioritize work and hire excellent full-time care for family

Since most organizations still expect professionals who want to move into positions of leadership to prioritize work over other life responsibilities, these are still the norms.

Michelle and Rob wanted to follow a different path. They wanted to be involved in raising their children, and they also needed two incomes. To accommodate these goals, both parents made changes at work, and both parents played an active role in the care of their children. Then, over time, both became leaders in their organizations.

The Third Path—Michelle and Rob wanted to pursue an integrated approach to work and family. With this approach, both parents redesign their work so they can prioritize their careers alongside plenty of time to care for their children and their relationship with each other.

Our ThirdPath Leader Guide introduces you to our amazing community of parents and the unique ways they combined professional ambition alongside time for family. We also reveal the secret ingredient—why having two parents work together around these goals creates a long-lasting way to achieve what you are looking for: time for all the life roles you care about, as a parent, lover, friend.

To learn more about how you can find a more satisfying way to integrate work and family, read Michelle and Rob's story to see what they discovered.

ON TRACK FOR A NEW KIND OF LEADER— MICHELLE AND ROB

When Michelle and Rob were expecting their first daughter, they began to look around for inspirational examples of people getting the most from both work and family.

At the time, they both worked as public accountants, and what they quickly noticed was that the majority of successful people in their line of work who were also parents were either mothers who had nannies or fathers whose wives didn't work outside the home.

Michelle and Rob knew that wasn't for them. They both wanted to be involved in raising their children. They also needed two incomes.

Instead, they decided that one of them would find a job that allowed for more family-friendly hours.

As it turns out, Michelle actually enjoyed her work in public accounting, whereas Rob did not. This made their decision an easy one. Rob sought new work that would allow him a more flexible schedule. Then together they could better manage the ups and downs of Michelle's schedule.

Two years later their second daughter was born, and, with a solid routine already in place, the transition into a family of four went smoothly. The girls attended daycare, and Rob, after going to work early in the mornings, would pick both children up around 4:00 pm and then care for them until

Michelle got home in time for dinner. But the year before their oldest was set to start kindergarten, things changed.

It happened suddenly. The family's plans for summer childcare were changed by an unexpected shift in the center's policy—their daughter was no longer eligible for care—and the routine care they had counted on for so many years, including during the summers, was no longer available to them.

Considering the different options, Michelle found herself thinking back to the summers of her youth and how pivotal they had been to her own childhood. Both of Michelle's parents had been teachers, and, in her experience, summers meant lazy afternoons filled with family and fun.

These memories shaped into an idea, a rather radical one, but she couldn't shake it. She wanted her daughters to have a summer like she used to know, and she wanted to be part of it. She decided she would ask for the summer off.

First, she broached the idea with Rob. Assuming her firm would go for it, there would certainly be a reduction in pay, and they had to make sure this was viable for the family finances. After deciding it was, they both started getting excited about Michelle's summer plans.

Would her firm feel the same way? Michelle approached her managing partners about adjusting her work schedule.

She knew the idea of taking a large chunk of time away from work to focus on family was unheard of at the firm. It took courage to be the first, and she had to be prepared for every possibility.

It helped that summers were generally a slower period at work. Michelle was a top employee, and the managing partners wanted to make sure they could keep her happy. Together they discussed the situation and decided the arrangement was a win-win. After that, Michelle was—most unexpectedly and most delightfully—able to spend the summer with her two girls much in the same way that her parents had done with her.

Meanwhile, her firm spent the summer merging with a bigger company. While her supportive managing partners were still part of the equation, they were no longer directly overseeing her position. That role fell to a new managing partner, who brought a different attitude about the arrangement.

When Michelle returned to work, she was refreshed and ready to re-engage with work. She was also determined to turn what had been a temporary fix into a permanent solution. Michelle approached her new manager about an 80% flex-year schedule that would allow her to work standard hours in the fall, longer hours during tax season, and then have two months off every summer.

The new partner was skeptical. He even took Michelle to a special lunch, during which he spent two hours explaining why her plan wasn't feasible. He thought the arrangement wasn't fair and that Michelle was trying to get out of doing her share of work. Michelle persisted, this time enlisting the help of the partners that had supported her before the merger, specifically the one who had proven a trusted mentor and confidant over the years.

She knew that getting him onboard would help in convincing the new managing partner to have an open mind and give the idea more consideration.

Luckily this worked, but the new managing partner only reluctantly agreed. Afraid that Michelle's arrangement would encourage others to do the same, he insisted that she keep the agreement a secret.

However, secrecy proved difficult. Michelle's coworkers did not know that she had taken a 20% reduction in salary to make it happen. They only knew that she was leaving the office earlier in the day, while they were not. The discomfort from this situation led Michelle to have serious doubts about continuing the arrangement. Several times she nearly gave up.

The only thing that kept her going was the positive impact her hard-fought schedule had on her family. She knew that time with her daughters, including the example she was setting for them, was worth it.

Then, as luck would have it, the secretive, work-first managing partner was replaced with someone much more supportive. In fact, the new and larger company the original company had merged with saw flexibility as a new important strategy for retaining the best and brightest workers. Suddenly Michelle's solution went from being a secret to something the company was excited to brag about.

Michelle stuck with her schedule, tweaking and adjusting as needed. Rob continued to do his share, especially during Michelle's busy season when the brunt of home and life responsibilities fell on him. And summers, with little work and lots of family, remained Michelle's focus for many years.

Preparing for the summer break, Michelle would make sure to have all the deliverables and questions wrapped up prior to leaving. She also learned a few tricks along the way. A few weeks before leaving for the summer, she would email all her clients to give them an opportunity to ask questions and make sure they knew that plans were in place during her absence. She sent similar emails to staff and partners, including specifics about her summer schedule, such as when she would be reachable and when she would not.

She also planned her kids' summers well in advance, making sure solutions were in place on days she would need to go into the office. She even improved her overall organizational approach. Michelle got smarter around delegation, preparing her subordinates and peers to make informed decisions without her.

Summer after summer, her routine grew smarter and smarter, which was good for her and her family but also good for her workplace. By delegating and training for her absence, she was able to become more of a mentor to her staff and create a stronger workforce. She set a pace of success and served as a positive example for her daughters, as well as an inspiration for other women in the firm—and men, too.

Today, the impact of more manageable hours and summers spent with her family has made Michelle a better worker. When at work, she is able to focus on the tasks at hand rather than the distractions of home, and when she is at home, she is less distracted by work.

In time Michelle was also asked to participate in the training to become a partner at her firm. Today she is the CFO of Independent Bank Group, and she continues to use her influence to encourage those around her to follow an integrated approach to work and life.

Her husband Rob has also become a ThirdPath Leader, managing one of the first virtual teams at his organization.

No doubt, they've also become role models to everyone around them.

BECAUSE OF THE SCIENCE OF WORK-LIFE INTEGRATION

Those who have successfully found a way to integrate work and life have discarded the outdated notion that a work-first and work-only approach is essential to business and the only route to success. Then, they reframed this binary assumption into one that recognizes that both work AND life matter.

In a world where we could work everywhere all the time, these leaders also learned that their commitment to their lives outside of work helps them become more efficient at work. And while technology gets its share of the blame, they strategically use it to harness a more manageable approach to work that benefits everyone involved.

Starting from the assumption that employees are giving their best effort at work—which most are willing to do—then we also have to assume there is a point of maximum capacity for every employee. Before the pandemic, too few organizations paid attention to this.

Instead, many were in a perpetual state of fire drills and chronic overwork, where everyone felt like they were being pulled in multiple directions. Problems arise when company goals constantly require employees to work over capacity. Or, as one of the progressive leaders in the ThirdPath community framed it, "If you constantly work a factory at 120% capacity, things are going to break down."

It also means that, even in organizations where employees receive seemingly progressive benefits like "unlimited vacation time," they probably aren't able to fully disengage from work when they take their vacations.

Two decades into teaching the science of work-life integration, we've learned that employees who practice an integrated approach develop important skills to help them improve how they work. They learn skills such as priority-setting, future-planning, strategic use of technology, creating routine focused work time, and setting triple-win boundaries—boundaries that are good for you, the work you do, and the people you work with.

This is why practicing an integrated approach was helpful when the pandemic hit and everyone's life was turned upside-down as schools and child care programs closed.

This guide will teach you the science of work-life integration: how it benefits you, your family, AND your organization. Look at the next page to learn why.

EPISODIC OR CHRONIC OVERWORK

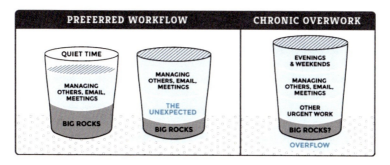

Are you experiencing "episodic" or "chronic" overwork?

- "Workflow" is the pace and quantity of work we do.
- A normal part of work includes experiencing busy and less busy periods of workflow—the two glasses on the left. We call a peak period of workflow "episodic" overwork.
- In too many organizations, professionals are in a perpetual state of managing "too much work." In order to complete assignments in a timely way, work spills into evenings, weekends, and even vacations. We describe this as "chronic" overwork—the glass on the right.

Benefits to organizations that promote reasonable "workflow":

- Employees stay focused on their "big rocks"—their most important work.
- Employees are encouraged to find routine "quiet time"—time for planning, thinking, writing, and other work that benefits from uninterrupted time.
- Employees "recharge" on weekends and return to work refreshed and creative.
- Employees use "slower" periods at work to re-prioritize what's important, put efficiencies in place, and plan for what's coming next.
- Teams learn that having a little more wiggle room allows them to better manage the unexpected.
- Over time, teams become increasingly skilled at proactively managing workflow and reducing the potential problems that can happen from chronic overwork.

Signs your organization may perpetuate chronic overwork:

- Your organization is constantly managing the next "fire drill."
- There is never time to put efficiencies in place to avoid future drills.
- "Flex" means work spills into evenings, weekends, vacations, and parental leave.
- Too often people feel exhausted and pulled in multiple directions.
- Employees who set limits at work feel guilty or are seen as lacking commitment.

BECAUSE IT WILL TRANSFORM HOW WE LIVE AND WORK

Are you saying I can have a better life AND change the world?

Yes, we are. Since founding ThirdPath Institute over twenty years ago, we've learned that the more people who follow this path—moving ahead in their careers while also creating plenty of time for family—the more leaders we will have to promote change for everyone.

Unfortunately, it's also very likely that the US will continue to lag behind other countries in creating progressive public policies in this arena.

Good public policy is essential for change. But we believe progressive leadership can be a catalyst that expedites the process of promoting work-life integration for all.

Following this approach, we all become more effective at getting our work done and having time to invest in the care of our loved ones. However, these benefits have a positive ripple effect that goes much farther, from the individual to the family to our workplaces to society as a whole.

In the past, managers had to be physically present to get work done, and, more often than not, they also had wives at home to care for their children.

But the world has changed. Today, this is no longer the best way to manage a global or distributed workforce or to keep up with changing technology. This is especially true when both men and women are interested in doing work and family differently.

Did you know that, with the right skills and mindset, almost any leadership position can be redesigned? The critical ingredient is the will to do so.

That's what we can learn from grandfather Ivan's story. Read on to see how leaders like Ivan—leaders who are taking a few calculated risks—can make a decision to change things for the better, for themselves, AND for their workplaces.

Ivan would also be the first to say his life has improved because of these changes and so would the world around him.

A LIFE CHANGING EXPERIENCE—GRANDPA IVAN

Shortly after Ivan's daughter had a child, the family discussed the potential childcare options available once maternity leave was over.

Ivan's wife volunteered to watch the baby one day per week, while the in-laws would cover two additional days, but there was still a hole in the schedule.

"I'll take a day," said Ivan.

"You'll take a day to do what?" replied the chorus.

While most would agree that Ivan is a kind and capable man, the truth was that he had never really spent time alone with a baby. Yes, he changed his share of diapers when his daughters were small, but the agreement between Ivan and his wife involved her staying home with the kids while Ivan worked. Much of their quality family time occurred around the dinner table, with the girls often staying up late to have a meal with their hardworking father.

Despite the fact that his wife and daughter had little faith in his ability to follow through with this plan, Ivan was assigned to Mondays.

Ivan also discussed this with his partners at his firm. Two, in particular, were skeptical. He told them, "If it's not working, let me know."

Ivan began to assign his team more responsibility, delegating so that he didn't have to be involved in every conversation. Fortunately, they were up to the task. They were a talented group. And "talented people," Ivan believed, "are likely to grow when given the opportunity."

Ivan also learned a few things himself. Initially, he believed, "Babies sleep a lot so I'll be able to work from home anyway." In time he had to come to terms with the fact that, while babies do sleep a lot, they seldom do so with any regularity, or in consecutive blocks of time.

Ivan's wife remained skeptical, and, since she was also home on Mondays, she offered her assistance.

"No," Ivan said. "This is my job."

Ivan was determined to create a relationship with his granddaughter, ensuring she would remember him forever. His daughters didn't have that opportunity with his parents since his parents both died when the girls were young. Ivan wanted things to be different for the next generation.

It didn't take long for him to learn what he didn't know and to adjust and tweak things, both at home and in the office. Soon, the new Monday become the regular Monday. It also became his favorite day of the week.

Two years later a grandson arrived, and Ivan added him into the mix. "I'm going to continue this Monday forever," he said.

That was eleven years ago, and while circumstances have changed as the kids have grown, Ivan still drives them to school every Monday. He then goes to the office for part of the day and returns to pick them up and take them back to his house, ending the day with a dinner with extended family.

His expanded flexibility has inspired positive change for the entire firm.

While the firm has always been supportive to staff, retaining many employees for decades, it has been Ivan's experience, paired with a generational push toward improved quality of life, that has helped introduce and encourage his firm to try new things.

Today the firm attracts top hires fresh from college, something he admits wasn't always possible.

There was a time when the best accounting students would go straight to the bigger firms after graduation, but Ivan's firm's growing support for work-life balance, instead of the industry standard of 50-60-hour workweeks, has made the firm far more appealing to recent college graduates. Or to individuals of any age, really.

Prior to the pandemic, the Los Angeles-area firm opened a satellite office to ease the impact of traffic on employee commutes. Once a month they also hosted Fun Friday for the entire staff to come together as a way to unwind and bond.

Ivan had no way of knowing over a decade ago that his professional life would be so shaped by his personal life, and yet it only took one leader trying something different to help the company appreciate the value of remote and flexible work.

Ivan said that, if not for his grandchidren, he isn't sure that his firm would have evolved at the rate that it has.

The changes fulfilled him both personally and professionally. Now Ivan is inspired to help others find their best self, in life, work, and everything.

NOTES

THE HARDEST CONVERSATION OF YOUR LIFE—AGAIN

It's a fact: couples trying to find their way on the ThirdPath Leader journey will get stuck. Their plans will get derailed, and there will be things that trip them up, be it a new baby, financial concerns, disagreeing with one's partner, asking for changes at work, or any number of potential obstacles, both expected and unforeseen.

Even in the most supportive of workplace environments, balancing work and life needs can be challenging. We are faced with constant change. Work changes, and kids get older, from the new parents' stage with its lack of sleep and experience (but also the wondrous and lovely opportunity to witness so much change in such a short period of time) to school years, teens, and beyond.

Change is constant. ThirdPath Leaders face it together through ongoing conversations and shared goals.

Some couples start on the same page; others do not. Some have conversations before having kids; others face marital strife in search of a focused plan. In time, all learn to work with their partners to develop skills around work redesign and parenthood.

What makes these conversations so hard? Everything.

From a fear of losing ground in one's career, the stress of disagreement and frustration in a partner, the challenge of drawing boundaries at work in order to have energy for family to determining what is really important and to figuring out how to have enough time AND money—the list of potential challenging conversations may feel endless.

Our twenty years of experience working with ThirdPath Leaders has taught us a variety of techniques to navigate these challenges, including having a solid Plan B just in case you become derailed from Plan A.

No matter the situation, whether implementing their preferred approach or following an alternate route, couples can always find answers that lead to their shared long-term goals.

Learning to have these conversations helps couples work together as a team to create the life they both want. The team approach also helps each person develop valuable skills that grow stronger as life and work keep changing. Take a look at our "Getting on the Same Page" visual. Which factors will help you create a team approach at home? Which ones will make it more challenging?

GETTING ON THE SAME PAGE—OVERVIEW

When creating your preferred approach to balancing work and family, begin by understanding each of your individual goals and experiences.

Once these are clear, use this to begin shaping a common plan.

Work and Career Redesign

How similar are you and your partner's **goals** around the amount of time you each want to spend at work?

Have you seen successful **integrated careers** in your line of work? How about for your partner?

Have you already had **personal success** flexing when, where, or how much you work? How about your partner?

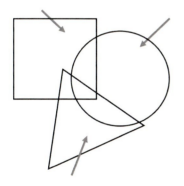

Family Redesign and Money

How **similar** are you and your partner's goals around the **time** you want a parent to provide care and the amount of childcare you want to use?

How important is it for both of you to contribute to the family's **finances**?

How important is it for you to create a **shared approach** to caregiving and household tasks?

Have you made choices around **spending, savings, and earnings** that support or impede your work/family balance goals?

Your Supervisor and Organization

How supportive is your **supervisor**? How about your partner's supervisor?

Are there any formal or informal **policies** that promote an "integrated" approach to work and life at your organization? How about for your partner?

Are there any **leaders** who model this approach in your organization? Or any men who model this approach? How about for your partner?

IT'S ABOUT GENDER, BUT IT'S NOT

Assumptions around gender, be they societal, cultural, or otherwise, often limit how couples share roles at work and home.

Women may assume that they will be the primary parent even though their partner is interested in sharing the responsibilities. Or both parents may consciously (or unconsciously) protect one parent's career—surprise, it's often the man's!—as a way to decrease the financial risk of working differently.

For families without children, it has become much more common to create non-traditional divisions of responsibilities. But once kids enter the picture, even same-sex families aren't immune to the consequences of stereotypes and gender-driven, role-based conflict.

That's because families need time, not just money, and this need smacks up against strong norms and assumptions about how to approach work and family.

People fear they won't be able to advance in their careers if they make changes at work to benefit home. After all, the folks at the top all seem to be work-focused and immune to the needs of home and family.

In fact, one modern twist in today's two-professional families is to have dad become the stay-at-home parent and mom continue with the big job. Bottom line: most couples struggle to think outside the box when it comes to reimagining work and family.

The leaders we've worked with weren't immune to these challenges.

But ThirdPath Leaders quickly learn that the key to their success is thinking outside the box—both around caregiving and when it comes to managing demanding careers.

We can see this in Shimul and Roger's story. While first making plans for a new baby, Shimul forgot that Roger could be part of the equation, even though both parents worked for the same company. It wasn't until Roger raised the issue that Shimul realized she didn't need to be solely responsible for solving their family's work and family needs.

Then, utilizing opportunities afforded to them by their employer, Shimul and Roger found a way to start their ThirdPath Leader journey together.

A FOOT IN EACH DOOR—ROGER AND SHIMUL

Roger and Shimul are still in the thick of it. Given that their kids are both under the age of ten, they are deep in the throes of the challenges that come from school calendars and work deadlines. But the confidence they gain from each other makes it all much more manageable.

Shimul and Roger both work for the same Fortune 500 company, and when they were expecting their first child, Shimul was trying to figure out how she could reduce her work hours to accommodate parenting while still remaining connected to her career.

Roger had his own thoughts. He had been inspired by the reduced work-week of Kelly, one of his previous bosses. He liked the way that she and her husband had both redesigned their work and shaped successful careers alongside a rewarding home life.

One day, finding Shimul particularly stressed about the situation, Roger reminded her that he worked for the same company and that he'd be happy to also request a reduced schedule. After discussing it, including the pay cut that would go with this plan, they both decided this would be the best option for their family.

"We didn't want to be all or nothing," said Shimul. "Having one of us stay home full-time was not for us, and working full-time while someone else raised our kids was also not for us."

"It's hard to see all of this when you're first starting out." Shimul added. "But ten years later, watching our friends truly struggle, I am so thankful we did what we did. At one point I did the math, and my pay has gone up 43% since our first child was born. That's clearly because I stayed in the workforce."

According to Roger, "A huge part of why this is fantastic is the ability to have one-on-one time with the kids, way more than in a 'traditional' setting. Plus, Shimul and I both have a good idea of what the other goes through. Sometimes it's great, sometimes it's horrible, and we understand why. We also know what work is like. I think we get each other more than we would otherwise."

Roger continued, "Where other parents face pressures from home, it's not hard for us to accommodate family life at all. For example, it's never good to have a sick kid, but in terms of being there for the child and this affecting our work schedule, it's not an issue at all. So much of it is having more time with the family. I can't imagine working 40, 50, 60 hours a week and not having this time with my kids. And I would also be taking that time away from Shimul. We've got ourselves set up to be very flexible and adaptable, and we've benefited so much from it."

MONEY, RISK, AND WORK-FIRST CAREERS

Most organizations promote a work culture that believes that the more hours employees work, the more they should be rewarded with raises, bonuses, and promotions. Unfortunately, this reinforces unhelpful gender norms both at work and at home.

For example, to pay off debt, many young people take high-paying jobs that have grueling work hours. Then, as plans for a family begin to take root, many feel trapped. They learn that the work-first workplaces they joined have narrowly defined assumptions around careers and what it takes to be successful. Things can get messy.

ThirdPath Leaders have learned that there are ways to combat this problem. They have proven that both parents can set boundaries at work and use their team approach to better manage any potential risk as they move ahead with their professional goals. Spoiler: It isn't easy. Risks can lead to discomfort. What happens when both parents push for changes at work? Will this lead to career suicide and a financial dead end?

Will and Teresa are a great example of a couple who took some risks, and, despite Will's workplace culture, were able to think outside the box and put their ideas into action.

It's a logical solution. Two people working toward the same goal allows for more support and flexibility. But you have to be courageous and stick up for your goals. Too often couples feel compelled to lower their goals at work or at home.

One way to begin the process is to assess how you are doing right now. How satisfied are you both around your current work-life coordinates? Your time as a couple? Your time to connect with your kids? Your time for fun and friends? The more couples develop a common vision, the more they will succeed in finding a new solution.

Most of our ThirdPath Leaders began their careers in organizations that were not supportive. Some went on to shape more supportive cultures elsewhere. Those who stayed figured out how to become ThirdPath Leaders despite all-consuming demands. See the next page to be inspired by how Will and Teresa pushed back at traditional gender roles and Will's work-first work culture, redesigning work to share childcare and later taking a six-month sabbatical.

What next steps do you want to take to further align your work and life goals? Check out our "Team at Home" exercise to help you get started.

TEAM AT HOME— YOUR CURRENT COORDINATES

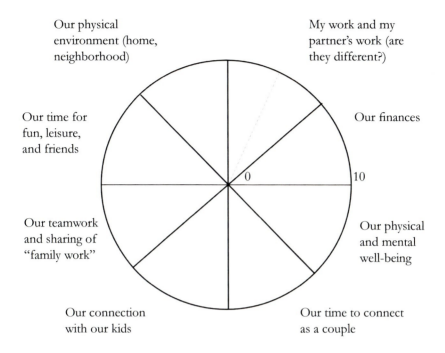

Our physical environment (home, neighborhood)

My work and my partner's work (are they different?)

Our time for fun, leisure, and friends

Our finances

Our teamwork and sharing of "family work"

Our physical and mental well-being

Our connection with our kids

Our time to connect as a couple

Team at Home Instructions

The eight sections in the above circle can all contribute to our sense of joy and satisfaction with our "Team at Home."

1. Work together to change, split, or rename any category so that it is meaningful for you.
2. Decide whether to work together to enter your responses or to work separately and then compare rankings when finished.
3. Taking the center of the wheel as 0 and the outer edge as 10, rank your level of satisfaction with each area by drawing a line to create a new outer edge—10 is very satisfied, 0 is very unsatisfied (see example).
4. The new perimeter of the circle represents your current "Team at Home" opportunities and challenges. How well-aligned are you and your partner? What area would you like to address first to achieve greater satisfaction as a couple?

Example

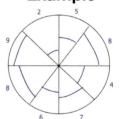

FOLLOWING THEIR NORTH STAR—WILL AND TERESA

Will's story starts with a plan, and that plan started with his wife Teresa. Years ago, when they were still dating, Teresa presented Will with a list of pros and cons, and, after Will reviewed each, Teresa simply stated, "I would like to marry you." Will said yes. "She has ideas," he is fond of saying. "And I implement them."

Will, by all accounts, is a workaholic, always on the phone, checking email, and making big decisions. He is good at what he does and has the title to prove it. He probably also has a nice office, but that isn't where you're likely to find him. "I integrate work and life," he says. "It's not a balance, but an integration. I work remotely from home a lot."

Although Will's company has made efforts to attract new employees, from offering more flexible schedules to relaxing the dress code, it retains its intensive work culture. There is a constant and steady flow of deadlines and deliverables to be met. There are clients to keep happy. Everyone is a Type A. Will is no exception.

Will's ability to work remotely gives him flexibility. This includes perks like allowing him to be present in aspects of family life that many of his coworkers miss. The exchange is time, with him staying up very late and waking up extremely early to get work done. "It's an ongoing struggle for Will," says Teresa. "It drains him."

At this point, perhaps you are wondering how Will is a ThirdPath Leader if he is always working, at home or elsewhere. Isn't that the issue we're trying to change?

Yes, which is where Will comes in. At a company that expects its employees to work late, on weekends and vacations, Will is a success story. He is the change.

When Teresa was expecting their first child, a son, she relayed to Will her first of many ideas. As a pediatrician, she had learned that life is short and fragile and that the window when children are at home is small and always closing. She wanted Will to adopt a compressed workweek, that is, four longer days on, with three days off. Doing so, combined with her working part-time, would allow the two of them to provide the majority of care for their son.

"One of the pros on her list was knowing I would be a good father," said Will. "We knew we both wanted to play a big role raising our kids."

Though the schedule was nearly unheard-of in a work-first setting, especially for men, his employer agreed. Everything was going to plan. More or less.

When Teresa was expecting their daughter, Will found himself pursued by a much bigger company. Will wasn't overly interested. He agreed to meet with them but found himself trying to sabotage the process by sharing concerns he thought were sure to be deal-breakers.

He wanted to maintain his compressed work week. They said that was fine. He explained that the timing was poor, that his wife was on bed rest, and they said not to worry. They increased his offered salary, assured proper insurance coverage, and provided paid paternity leave. He couldn't say no.

The day after Will and Teresa returned home from the hospital with the new baby, they were visited by Will's new employers. In one hand they offered their hearty and generous congratulations, and in the other they described a major proposal that they needed Will to write, immediately.

Paternity leave became a part-time thing where Will helped his family by day and drafted the proposal by night. "Is this what it's going to be like?" asked Teresa. He didn't know. Will found himself secretly hoping the proposal wouldn't be accepted, afraid of what it might mean for his compressed schedule and the plan of being present in the lives of his children. When they won the contract, everyone was happy, but Will had his doubts

Still, everything worked out. The routine righted itself. The client became an anchor in a new business line, with Will running point. Will spent Fridays with the children.

A few years passed, and Teresa, who had been working part-time, knew that her company's financial issues would soon result in the need for her to find employment elsewhere. After leaving the job, she had another idea. She had always wanted to take a cross-country trip. It turns out that this was something Will had always dreamed about too. "I'm sure I can get two weeks of vacation," Will said. Teresa showed him her proposed inerary. It had sixty-six stops. "You'll need five or six months," she said. He countered with four weeks. She didn't budge. He thought perhaps he could get the company to agree to two months—after all, he had earned it.

Teresa stood her ground. Her idea was five or six months, and she needed Will to implement the plan. Will began running the idea by trusted friends, coworkers, clients, and neighbors. Every single one of them thought it was a great plan.

His colleagues were happy to take his lucrative clients, and his clients were supportive, as long as they were left in capable hands. His boss was also supportive, agreeing to a six-month sabbatical, despite there not being a formal policy in place. His boss' one stipulation? Will needed to get client approval and check his email daily. "It's all taken care of," Will said.

The school provided the curriculum for the kids, and Teresa taught lessons in the back of the RV while Will drove, hitting every dot on the map. "Then we'd pull into the next national park," said Will, "and the real learning started." 15,000 miles later, the kids were sad to see it end. They all were.

IMPOSSIBLE JOBS—MANAGING TOO MUCH WORK

Why do so many leaders appear to be workaholics? Because as leaders, there is no limit to how much work they can take on. In addition, most people don't learn good boundary-setting skills. And most organizations, as we've learned, discourage boundary-setting. But without an ability to set limits around work, the tendency to overwork gets worse and worse.

Even ThirdPath Leaders can get caught in the cycle of chronic overwork. The pressure of the tide—managing the ebb and flow of work—can sometimes feel extremely challenging.

When this happens, ThirdPath Leaders re-apply the tools they've learned to make an impossible job more possible—whether it's creating regular uninterrupted time for focused work, proactively managing peak periods of work, or learning when to delegate.

Unfortunately, leaders who work in chronically overworked workplaces may feel that the ability to set limits at work or that their success in building a team to better delegate their work is impossible. Instead, everyday fire drills make investing in a more planful use of time outside their reach.

Taming workflow—the pace and quantity of work we manage—is at the core of each ThirdPath Leader's success. It also helps us become better employees, parents, AND leaders.

ThirdPath Leaders use a combination of integration skills and strong teams at work to think ahead about what they can AND cannot take on. Then, they combine this with
increased flexibility from their team at home.

In short, this "team approach" of setting collective boundaries is great for business. The collective effort also helps everyone better navigate the constantly evolving challenges and opportunities that come their way.

Whether you are in a supportive environment or an overwhelming work-first workplace, there are strategies you can use to hold on to your work and family goals.

How is your current workflow impacting your work effectiveness? Take our survey to find out.

TAMING WORKFLOW

Workflow is the pace and quantity of work you do. When workflow constantly feels like a fire hose, both our work and our lives suffer.

Take a look at the below questions. Which one best describes you—the one on the left or right?

Improving How We Work

1= Left option describes me; 5 = Right option describes me

Sometimes the whole day disappears before I can take a break from work.	1 2 3 4 5	I take breaks between tasks, sometimes even taking a walk outside.
My work routinely spills into evenings and weekends.	1 2 3 4 5	On workdays I have time to focus on my most critical work.
My list of "most important work" keeps changing and/or getting longer.	1 2 3 4 5	I know what tasks I need to prioritize and what I can complete more slowly.
Every day, week, month feels as busy or busier then the last..	1 2 3 4 5	Though not always predictable, I have less busy times at work.
The stress of work spills into home and creates frustration and resentment.	1 2 3 4 5	We have routines at home that help us cope with busier periods at work.
I am often distracted by thoughts about work during non-work time.	1 2 3 4 5	More often than not, I am able to fully turn off work when away from work.
Work is so draining I don't have time for a number of important life tasks.	1 2 3 4 5	I have time and energy to do the life activities most important to me.
I have no time to implement new ideas for becoming more efficient at work.	1 2 3 4 5	My team members and I use slower periods at work to address inefficiencies.
When sent a curve ball, I quickly begin to feel overwhelmed.	1 2 3 4 5	I have time to stop, reflect, and respond creatively when the unexpected happens.
The spillover of work while on vacations makes me doubt the value of taking one.	1 2 3 4 5	Even during the pandemic, I've taken time away from work to unplug and recharge.

Notice how we think smarter and make better decisions when we push back at chronic overwork and take time to recharge!

SWIMMING AGAINST THE CURRENT

We've talked about the obvious workplace obstacles around gender stereotypes, work first organizations, and financial risks—issues that are all too familiar. Now, it's time to discuss something nobody wants to think about: people give up.

Following an integrated career path can feel hard.

It can feel like society doesn't want men to be actively involved fathers or that work can never be rearranged in such a way to support quality family life. Saying "no" to work is hard. More than one of our ThirdPath Leaders has told us, "It's easier to just let work take over."

Remember Michelle? When Michelle was in public accounting, she often had a crazy workload leading up to April 15th (Tax Day), but even during her busy season she didn't want work to take over her life.

Instead, Michelle got smarter. She and Rob hired more help at home. She also discovered the benefits of doing a couple of hours of "quiet work" in the morning before leaving for the office. In short, she learned to better manage the difficult times and to try to avoid bad habits, rather than to adopt them.

That's her success story, but to get there she had to learn the lessons only failure can teach. One year in particular, work was especially demanding. Despite her attempts to the contrary, she felt like she was becoming a workaholic and she wasn't sticking to her path. She nearly gave up.

Luckily, she was part of the ThirdPath community—a group of like-minded people who understood that going through a challenging period didn't mean Michelle had given up on her goals. Instead, she needed to find new answers and new inspiration.

Inspiration is different for everyone. It can come from the smallest things, swaddled and smiling, to the plans of a passionate partner who helps design a life-changing adventure. Inspiration is like that.

When we are facing tough odds, inspiration helps us stay on track.

Yes, there will be trial, error, and self-doubt. But today, you can get the support you need from the ThirdPath community and the parents who came before you.

Barriers

NOTES

CREATING A TEAM AT HOME

ThirdPath Leaders learn how to get on the same page and hold each other gently accountable as they work together to define and reach for their respective professional and family goals.

Together they design their preferred plan and reconcile their differences.

How will both partners contribute to family finances? Do they both have the same idea about what's the right amount of childcare? Do they know how much they want to spend (time, money, energy) on work versus other aspects of their life? Are they prepared for meeting the needs of their kids and how these needs will change over time?

The ability to create a team at home helps couples get smart about setting limits around work, helps them create time and energy for both work and family, and creates a unified front when it comes to finances—both earning and spending.

Getting on the same page is what makes it all work. It's the secret sauce.

Each couple's solution will look different, but they all share a common thread—a similar ability to support each parent as they flex around predictable and unpredictable changes. Through this give and take, couples create a deep bond and enjoy the benefits of having two parents become equally skilled in the care of their families and supporting each other to succeed in their professional goals.

Getting on the same page may be the secret sauce, but it also takes a lot of work. Couples will face curveballs, and lots of them. But together they can continue to work as a team, never losing sight of their collective goals.

We call these collective goals a family's North Star.

It's exactly what it sounds like, the goal to which each roadmap leads. Each family may have a different North Star—some more focused on equal roles, some more focused on family time—but defining one's own North Star is crucial. And sharing the same North Star with one's partner is even more so.

Every family has different needs and different solutions. There is no right or wrong answer, but there is a better way to find the right path for each family.

What is your North Star?

YOUR FAMILY'S "NORTH STAR"

1. **How important is it that both parents contribute towards the family's finances?**

   None   Part-Time   Full-Time
   Myself   1   2   3   4   5
   I think my partner's score would be: _____

2. **What do you feel is "the right" amount of childcare for your work-family solution?**

   None   Part-Time   Full-Time
   Myself   1   2   3   4   5
   I think my partner's score would be: _____

3. **How important are your goals for yourself around the work you do and/or your career?**

   None   Part-Time   Full-Time
   Myself   1   2   3   4   5
   I think my partner's score would be: _____

4. **How important is it for you to develop an "equal" solution or share things 50-50?**

   None   Part-Time   Full-Time
   Myself   1   2   3   4   5
   I think my partner's score would be: _____

5. **How important is it for you to have plenty of time as a family, couple time, self time, and/or time to be involved in your community?**

   None   Part-Time   Full-Time
   Myself   1   2   3   4   5
   I think my partner's score would be: _____

6. **How willing are you to trade time at work and income to create time for these priorities?**

   None   Part-Time   Full-Time
   Myself   1   2   3   4   5
   I think my partner's score would be: _____

LAUNCHING AN INTEGRATED CAREER

Though the third path journey starts at home, it also requires a new mindset at work, accepting that no matter how many hours a person works, there will always be more to do. Adopting this mindset helps people realize and then anticipate the fact that that their desire to have time for life outside work helps them work smarter and that that's better for everyone.

The skills required to follow the third path mindset include:

- **Self-Discipline**: Focusing on the present moment and getting work done despite distractions, whether or not you're doing your favorite task.
- **Prioritization**: Making trade-offs and understanding that you need to communicate them to everyone involved. This will likely include a discussion with your partner at home as well.
- **Agility and Future Planning**: Anticipating events that impact either life or work and proactively making changes to manage them. Planning for peak periods of work and making changes at work and at home to better manage them.
- **Strategic Use of Technology**: Using technology to proactively manage information-sharing and workflow, including when working remotely.

Each skill provides the building blocks for the two most essential skills:

- **Creating Routine Quiet Time**: Scheduling time for reflection and strategic thinking allows tasks to be accomplished efficiently and is essential for future planning. Self-discipline is required to book this time and avoid distractions.
- **Setting Personal Boundaries**: Keeping your focus on work you are uniquely qualified to do. Finding ways to delegate, say no, or go slow to lower priority work that is of less value to your organization.

Are there risks in setting limits at work to create time and energy for family? Yes. There will be moments you need to push back at managers who changed their minds or to educate a new manager unaware of the previous agreement. But when you start by first getting clear about your family's goals, you'll find more courage to ask for the changes you want at work—especially when both you and your workplace will benefit.

Read on to see how Bryan and Lisa let this mindset guide them when they both changed to a four-day work week to care for their new baby. Then use our "Courage Comes from a Strong 'Core'" exercise to see how you can support each other to reach for your goals.

COURAGE COMES FROM A STRONG "CORE"

Asking for change for your flex goals can be hard. Getting clear about your own goals and your goals as a family first will increase success in surfacing and planning for any potential external challenges.

Step 1: Before asking for any changes at work, take a quick look at the "internal factors." Do any look particularly challenging?

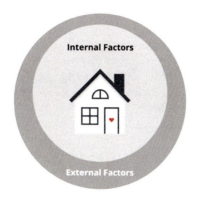

Step 2: Answer each "external factor" question.
Which might create the biggest obstacle to change? Which might provide the biggest opportunity?

Internal Factors

- How clear are you about what's important to you both at work and at home?
- How skilled are you at approaching work in a new way to have time and energy for family?
- How aligned are you both in achieving your preferred work-family goals? Are you also in agreement on your backup plan, just in case?
- Can you afford your preferred work-family goals and your backup plan?
- Do you have enough support to put your goals into action?

External Factors

- Do others in your organization flex and/or work reduced hours? What do your colleagues expect from a "team player"?
- Do any of the leaders or managers in your organization model taking time for their lives outside of work? What does your boss model?
- How do the needs of your clients or customers impact how everyone manages their work-life balance?
- Are there any formal and/or informal flex policies that would support your goals?

Step 3: How can you shape your request into a "triple win"—good for you, good for getting your work done, AND good for the colleagues and clients you work with? Would a pilot period help as a first step?

MANAGING RISK BY BUILDING IN BUFFERS— BRYAN AND LISA

Bryan and Lisa knew they wanted to have children. This meant they needed a plan, and planning would require good communication. Luckily, this was work they were both committed to doing. In fact, they had committed to doing it long before their first child was born.

One of the first decisions they made was to buy a house they could afford on one income. The realtor kept showing them homes in a fancier neighborhood. But Bryan and Lisa knew that living below their means would be critical to helping their unconventional ideas become a reality.

They also started saving when Lisa became pregnant so they could both take advantage of the time allotted by the Family and Medical Leave Act to support each other.

Once Lisa became pregnant, it was time for both of them to implement a four-day work week. In bold style, Bryan went to his boss and explained that after paternity leave, he would shift to a four-day work week for 80% pay. While having this conversation Bryan signaled both that he was willing to make sure the solution worked well for his company and also that the change in schedule wasn't open for negotiation.

This was new territory for both Bryan and Lisa and for the company.

Bryan shared, "At work, some of the people were surprised at what I was doing. And who knows, maybe I would have been promoted earlier if I had worked five days. But Lisa and I both knew there could be tradeoffs when equally valuing work and family and that we would be comfortable making them."

Bryan added, "I also knew the benefits of having balance in my life. If I got promoted, what would that mean? Just more money, a bigger house, and spending more money."

Fortunately, having been with the company for a while helped ease the novelty of Bryan's request, and the company was open to the change.

A few years into this new routine, Bryan realized he was ready for more challenging work. He had been with the company for seventeen years. Some of the work Bryan was now involved in was no longer as engaging so Bryan, with Lisa's support, decided it was time to look for a different job.

When Bryan began to explore his prospects, he was committed to taking his four-day workweek with him. During his job search, the market was hot, and even with the requirement of a four-day workweek, Bryan was offered three different jobs. The increased competition for talent also meant when he went back to his boss with plans to change jobs, he was immediately offered more money and more interesting projects in an effort to retain him. It was an offer Bryan couldn't pass up.

With work they both enjoyed and a second son added to the mix, Bryan and Lisa continued living the life they had always dreamed of. But about a year and a half later the market tanked, and Bryan found himself laid off and looking for work.

The funny thing about looking for employment when the market is bad is that companies are less likely to be flexible and to entertain ideas like Bryan's, despite the fact that they could save money by doing so. Even companies that had been previously open to four-day workweek were no longer willing to offer it.

Bryan tried pointing out the business logic of investing in him. "You're getting just as much value from me but paying 80%. It's a good deal for you." Instead, companies said the jobs were too demanding. They needed him all the time. A 60-hour work week was the norm. It simply couldn't be done in less.

Bryan and Lisa knew better. They both had a track record of meeting demanding deadlines that also supported time for life, but the companies Bryan was talking to were no longer interested in learning a new approach.

Luckily, Bryan and Lisa had always believed that money was important, but so was time, and they had structured their lives to build buffers in both. Bryan explained, "We had always managed our finances to allow flexibility and choice so that if one of us wanted to make a career change or lost a job, we could accommodate this change."

Bryan held on to his goal of looking for an organization that would support his four-day schedule. Because of the couple's careful budgeting, he could do it without having the anxiety of finances derailing the plan.

Eventually, not only did Bryan find a job that agreed to his schedule, he was also offered a position with growth opportunity. "I knew the CEO," Bryan said. "He knew I could do it. For the first time I would come in with a bigger title: director."

"When I was a kid, my dad came home, had dinner, and then went back to work. There wasn't a lot of time with him." Then unexpectedly, Bryan's dad died in his early sixties, and suddenly the plans to be more engaged in his life outside of work evaporated. Both experiences left a lasting impression on the choices Bryan would make in his own life.

"I have found so much joy in being a parent." Bryan says, "A sense of appreciation and closeness, because of the time I have spent with my boys."

He also credits Lisa for having the vision to start him on this plan and for the encouragement to help him stay on track. For the record, Lisa's pretty happy with him, too.

BUILDING IN BREATHING ROOM

Too many families hit the ground running on Monday, cram in a full day of work, then switch to caring for the kids, supervising homework, doing the dishes, and paying the bills. Then they do the whole thing again the next day and the day after that.

When weekends become a time to catch up on errands because there is no time during the week, the pace becomes exhausting for everyone. This is what it is like to be on the gerbil wheel of life, as unforgiving as it is constant.

People need time for work, but they also need time for home, self, and community, as well as time to recharge. Recharge time gives you time to breathe. Thankfully, there are many ways to create recharge time.

Recharge time also gives you the space to contemplate the big picture view: where you are going and what's around the corner. It helps us get smarter about managing our lives in the moment, facing the inevitability of children growing up and creating a more flexible approach to integrating work and family. With a team approach at home, parents work together to create more buffer time. Doing this helps them work together to consider bigger changes, while retaining their priorities, like time as a couple, self-care, and exercise.

Here are a few steps you can take to get off the gerbil wheel:

- **Plan Ahead**: Use a common calendar to better manage planned and unplanned changes. Do you have a network of support you can rely on to pinch hit or swap care? Is there a creative way to plan for this support going forward?
- **Extra Support**: What kind of support can you use to better manage home responsibilities? House cleaner? Lawn care? Groceries delivered? Can you involve the kids in meals and cleaning?
- **Time for Self**: Have you found a successful way to set up routine self-time? Taking turns having one parent be in charge of family can free up the other parent for some much-needed time for self or time to connect with friends.
- **Couple Time**: Too often the needs of the couple get lost while balancing the demands of work and family. Families do better when couples take care of their relationship. What could you do to create a little time together as a couple?

Take a look at the next page to better understand some of the challenges that can get in the way of recharge time.

CREATING RECHARGE TIME!

There are many challenges to creating "recharge time." Which impact you?

- Age of Children: Every stage of parenthood brings joys and challenges. What do you find most energizing or energy-depleting at this life stage?
- Work Demands: If work leaves you exhausted, you have less time and energy for other life interests. Is it time to set better boundaries at work?
- Life Demands: We all have the same 24-hour day. What's negotiable and non-negotiable? Can you put off that renovation project until life calms down?
- Back to Basics: A good night's sleep and routine exercise are probably the first essential steps of self-care. How satisfied are you with these two activities at this point in your life?
- Extra Planning and Support: Can you create a common calendar to help you better manage planned and unplanned changes in your life? Would paying for additional support help create more recharge time? Can your children help out?

As children get older and by being careful not to over schedule, we can all become more successful creating time for the things that most energize us.

What are the top three challenges you would like to change?
What do you want to create more time for?

APPROACHING FAMILY NEEDS TOGETHER

When you are balancing work and the care of an infant, it's hard to imagine that the needs of your family will change over time. Sleepless nights seem like they will last forever, but one day your baby will become a preschooler (and eventually a teenager!)

In short, no matter which path you pick—the first, the second, or the third path—it will inevitably include change, in both planned and unexpected ways.

ThirdPath Leaders learn to anticipate these changes and work together to plan for the next stage of parenthood.

Some of these responsibilities, such as childcare, eldercare, and food on the table, are non-negotiable. You can hire help to manage all of this, but hiring help alone doesn't necessarily give you enough breathing room.

To find the best solution, ThirdPath Leaders work together to decide: what's the right amount of help? How do we make sure we get enough sleep? Do we need to renegotiate our work flexibility? How can we ensure that we have recharge time?

Having both parents engaged as they meet the changing needs of family creates teamwork, empathy, and greater flexibility.

Working as a team means you and your partner deeply know and understand your child and develop unique ways to play with, care for, and interact with your child. Together, you will develop a larger, more flexible set of tools for caring for your child today and as they get older. You also better appreciate that job's pleasures and challenges.

Working as a team also means you share the experiences of being a working parent, the ups and downs of working with colleagues and bosses and handling work satisfactions and stresses. In addition, it increases your flexibility in managing both planned and unplanned changes.

Over time, you and your partner will likely become one of your most trusted resources as you strategize next steps at work and at home.

Take a look at our Family Stages diagram. Which stage are you experiencing right now? What's around the corner? How will sharing in the care of your family increase the joys in your life?

FAMILY STAGES—JOYS AND CHALLENGES

It's hard to imagine how quickly your children will change, but they will, and each stage will bring many joys and challenges.

As you imagine what's around the corner, remember that new parents or families expecting another child often organize their work-family "care schedule" around the needs of their youngest child. Those with school-aged children will likely need to revise their schedules again to meet the needs of teenagers.

New Family Delights

- Huggable
- Affectionate
- Easy to redirect
- Intense wonder and responsiveness to the experiences that surround them.

School-Age Wonders

- Can get in and out of the car on their own
- Can play with friends independently
- Bedtimes become more routine
- Can begin to help around the house

Teen Amazements

- Can plan own day
- Can help at home
- Can manage own homework
- May earn income for self or family
- More self-reliant, even on vacations

New Family (Children ages 0 -2)	Young School-Age Family (Children ages 3,4 or 5-12)	Teen Family (Children 13-18)
Shorter Stage	*Longer Stage*	*Shorter Stage*
Care every day	Care before/after school (or preschool) + summer	

New Family Challenges

- Lack of sleep
- Need for constant adult supervision (including when you are "on vacation")
- Finding quality part-time or full-time childcare
- Balancing work and the needs of a sick child

School-Age Challenges

- School closings—planned and unplanned
- Balancing work and the needs of a sick child
- The need to organize care over summers
- Unexpected challenges; best friend leaving or a difficult match with a teacher

Teen Challenges

- Influences from peer group around school, drinking, dating, and the need "to own the latest thing"
- Continued need to organize care over the summers
- Doesn't like school
- The extra support required to help them get into college

PRIORITIZING TIME ALONGSIDE MONEY

As a society, we have been trained to believe that more money is always better. ThirdPath Leaders turn this assumption upside down. Instead, they ask: "Can we design a financial solution that allows us the time we want, not just the money we need?"

For many families, the time-money tradeoff is a luxury they can't afford, but for those who can make such a choice, there are many rewards. By getting clear about life priorities, being intentional around spending, and creating financial buffers, ThirdPath Leaders create more time for the things they really love. But it's not just how much a family earns that's in question. Many families fear setting limits at work could be risky for their family's future financial health.

The way to manage this risk is to follow a "life-centered approach" to finances.

A life-centered approach to family finances is something we learned from one of the fathers we know who does financial planning with young families. He encourages parents to think about the time they want for different things—family, partner, kids, and other highly valued non-work activities—then to use these "life goals" to become more intentional about how to manage earning and spending income to achieve them.

Being conservative around spending can help you afford to use time in a way that is most aligned with your values. It also helps you better manage unexpected unemployment or the need to temporarily reduce your work hours.

Our ThirdPath Leaders apply the life-centered approach to family finances in a variety of ways. As one mom explained, "Live at or below your means, but never above your means." Another father told us, "Avoid the assumption that the person who earns more should work more. Instead, find solutions that advance the family's needs and each parent's professional goals as a whole."

Just as there are different "North Stars" for families, there is also a wide range of ways ThirdPath Leaders "balance" the competing needs of time and money.

We all need money to live, but the amount depends on how much we spend and save, how much debt we have, and our values. With reflection, conversation, and visualization, each of us can find our unique, life-centered financial equation. What is the right money, time, and family-care equation for you?

MONEY, TIME, AND FAMILY CARE

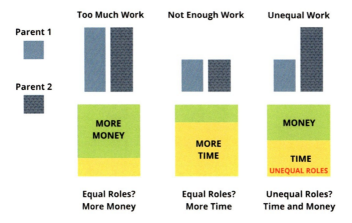

Our decisions around how much paid work we do, how much family care we provide, and who does the paid work and family care are influenced by multiple factors. To begin to better understand what you want in the future, take a look at what's going well right now.

Children
How old are your children? No kids? Ask a family who is a role model: how would they answer the following questions?

Family
What's something you like about how you are approaching the time you have to care for your children and family? What do you like about the role your partner is playing?

Work
What's something you like about how you are approaching the time you spend at paid work? What about your partner's approach?

Money
What's something you like about how you and your partner are contributing to your family's financial needs—either by earning income, keeping expenses low, or by creating a financial buffer through savings?

Think anew!
What are one or two things you would like to change around you and your partner's approach to work, family, and money?

KEEPING AN EYE ON YOUR LIFE AND CAREER

Up until now, we've given you the chronological approach to your road map: it starts with creating a team at home; then you launch your integrated career. You also make sure you leave enough breathing room and that you are smart about money. But then there is the monkey wrench (or two).

Life unfolds in unpredictable ways: birth, death, marriage, divorce, promotions, unemployment, illness, a new job, education, eldercare, plus so many more. Any one of these changes has the power to greatly influence your roadmap for better and sometimes worse, and the truth is, most of us will experience several items from this list. Given this truth, here's the approach our ThirdPath Leaders use to manage constant change.

Work-Life Integration Process

Create Time to Reflect
- Make the most of slower periods at work and home to assess what you are doing and develop fresh ways to focus on what's most important.
    - Rethink priorities, find efficiencies, advance more realistic goals.
    - Take time to journal or "think big" with your partner about your work and life goals.
- When things are extra busy, create "no work" weekends or Saturdays.
- Feeling pressed for time? Even a short walk where you turn your thoughts away from the task you are working on can help you refocus and recharge.

Make Changes Outside of Work
- Develop a clear sense of highly valued non-work activities. Create time for family, friends, and activities that are of equal (or greater) importance than the work you do.
- Get gentle support from the people who are closest to you—spouse, friend, family member, coach—to prioritize non-work activities.
- During the times of year that work and/or home are especially busy, avoid taking on extra projects and get extra help.

Make Changes at Work
- Create a supportive work team. Develop everyone's expertise around managing and predicting "workflow"—the pace and quantity of work. Find ways to support each other to flex and to work together to manage busier periods.
- Keep perspective. Are you in an organization where everyone is chronically overworked? Change may be harder. But don't forget, chronic overwork is not good for anyone and it decreases work effectiveness.

Experiment, Learn, Repeat
- With every change we are given another chance to experiment and learn.

BEFORE YOU KNOW IT, KIDS GROW UP

Whether you are a new parent or parent of a child about to start school or pre-school, there is no better time than the present to begin shaping your third path journey.

How do you want to start your journey? Caring for INFANTS AND TODDLERS.

Lisa & Bryan
Both worked a four-day work week. They used three days of childcare on the other days.

Roger & Shimul
Both worked reduced hours and shared care the rest of the week.

Will & Teresa
Will worked a compressed work week, Monday through Thursday. Teresa worked reduced hours on Wednesday, Friday, and Saturday. They used childcare on Wednesdays.

Ivan
Cared for his granddaughter on Mondays. Can extended family members play a role for you?

Here's how things changed (or didn't) during the SCHOOL-AGED YEARS

Lisa & Bryan
Both continued the same schedule during the early school year, using the same childcare center for summer care.

Roger & Shimul and Will & Teresa
Both continued their same schedule, including in the summers.

Michelle & Rob
Michelle adopted an 80% flex-year schedule, taking two months off over the summer. Rob shifted his work day, starting early, and picking up the children by 4:00 pm.

Variation—Chris & Dave
They hired a nanny to help with three days of after-school care and three full days of care during the summer.

Want to better understand how to start shaping your own unique third path? Take a look at the exercise on the next page.

GETTING ON THE SAME PAGE—EXERCISE

Complete the below survey questions with your partner—maybe even separately to begin with. Compare your answers. Where are you most aligned?

Work and Careers: Exploring your goals around the role of work in your lives.

Managers and Organizations: Recognizing the role your supervisor and organization play, both for you and your partner.

Family and Money: Rethinking family responsibilities and creating time for the life you want.

Family Redesign and Money　　Your Response

- How similar are your goals around the time you want to spend with family and use paid childcare?

  Similar　　　　　Divergent
  1　　2　　3　　4　　5

- How similar are your goals around how you want to share caregiving and household tasks?

  Similar　　　　　Divergent
  1　　2　　3　　4　　5

- Have you made choices around spending, savings, and earnings that support or impede your work/family balance goals?

  Support　　　　　Impede
  1　　2　　3　　4　　5

Work Redesign

- How similar are your goals around the amount of time you each want to work?

  Similar　　　　　Divergent
  1　　2　　3　　4　　5

- Have you already had some success flexing when, where, or how much you work?

  More Success　　Less Success
  1　　2　　3　　4　　5

- How about for your partner: have they had some success?

  More Success　　Less Success
  1　　2　　3　　4　　5

Your Workplace

- How supportive is your supervisor?
- Are there formal or informal policies that promote a "balanced" or "integrated" approach to work and life?

  Very Supportive　No Support
  1　　2　　3　　4　　5
  Formal Policies　No Policies
  1　　2　　3　　4　　5

- Are there leaders who role-model an integrated approach at work?

  Many　　　　　　None
  1　　2　　3　　4　　5

Your Partner's Workplace

- How supportive is your partner's manager?
- Are there formal or informal policies that promote a "balanced" or "integrated" approach to work and life?

  Very Supportive　No Support
  1　　2　　3　　4　　5
  Formal Policies　No Policies
  1　　2　　3　　4　　5

- Are there leaders who role-model an integrated approach at work?

  Many　　　　　　None
  1　　2　　3　　4　　5

NOTES

INTEGRATION FOR YOUR WHOLE TEAM

The mindset you develop following the third path means that, when you are promoted into a leadership position, you will be more skilled at being a leader who promotes an integrated approach for your entire team.

In fact, there are many skills you will develop today that will help you become a better leader tomorrow. Here are just a few of them:

- Your understanding that you can't get it all done yourself helps you foster strong relationships so together you can accomplish what's most important.
- Your strength with planning and priority-setting will help you set more realistic deadlines with your team.
- The skills you learn turning off work while on vacation will help you encourage others to do the same.
- Your ability to create routine "quiet" or focused work time will help you deal with more complicated tasks, including effective delegation.
- Your enjoyment of technology-free time will help you become a role model for others to use technology more strategically.
- Your appreciation for the ways that setting boundaries creates time that allows you to think smarter and be more creative will help you understand the bottom-line benefits of work-life integration for all.

Anticipate the future	Build strong relationships
Plan and prioritize	Manage expectations
Cultivate self-discipline	Create a sense of reciprocity
Create quiet work time	Design strategic delegation
Use technology strategically	Promote two-way flex
Set personal boundaries	Set collective boundaries

Read on to see how the journey you begin today will help you become a new kind of leader and role model to everyone around you.

THIRDPATH LEADERS HELP THEIR TEAMS BY:

Building Strong Relationships

Building strong relationships helps everyone get their work done more effectively. Doing this requires seeing the opportunity of including others in the process and letting go of doing everything yourself. By building strong relationships, leaders create more opportunities for problem-solving when there are conflicting goals. It also creates a sounding board and network of support while managing work and life.

Managing Expectations

Proactively managing expectations helps maintain a positive environment and ensures that the "right" work is done in the "right" amount of time. It also reduces conflict by defining outcomes, setting clear expectations, and ensuring that these are mutually understood right from the start. Ultimately, managing expectations helps reduce the possibility of overpromising outcomes and doing unnecessary work.

Creating a Sense of Reciprocity

Mutual support greases the wheels. It enables one person to cover for another when the unexpected arises. It creates a loop of reinforcement, making strong relationships even stronger and developing resilience within the team as employees gain strength from their combined effort. Trust and reliability grow, all within a culture of flexibility in which coworkers back each other up or join together when someone is in need.

Designing Strategic Delegation

Effective delegation requires an understanding of the entire team's priorities, skills, and goals. When done effectively, delegation provides an opportunity to increase the skills of more junior employees, while freeing up the leader to focus on strategic work they are uniquely qualified to do. There may be an upfront investment, but this yields significant long-term benefits for everyone.

Promoting Two-Way Flex

Flexibility is mutual: it's a manager allowing for the unexpected personal issue and the individual allowing for the occasional late-night call. Flexibility allows a leader to adjust in real-time when expectations cannot be met due to unforeseen circumstances, and it opens doors to new opportunities and new information. Flex doesn't mean "anything goes." Instead, flex promotes creativity within boundaries set by the leader and team.

Setting Collective Boundaries

Setting boundaries continues to be one of the most important skills for supporting flex AND integrated lives. This helps team members better understand their essential responsibilities versus tasks that can be done at a slower pace. Negotiating this both at the individual- and team-level develops buy-in, reduces conflict, and builds stronger relationships. It also allows teams to work at a higher level of performance.

INTEGRATION ACROSS THE LIFE CYCLE

We hope our **ThirdPath Leader Guide** has shown you how our lives at work and our lives outside of work are connected and how the choices and actions we take in one area greatly impact the other. We also hope it's shown you how committing to an integrated life helps you become a new kind of leader and how doing so benefits your company and the teams you manage.

Becoming a ThirdPath Leader won't inoculate you from the need to engage in hard conversations, make tough choices, and deal with impossible jobs or from the feeling that you are sometimes swimming against the current.

However, each time you apply what you've learned, you will strengthen your skills and confidence in your ability to follow an integrated path. This becomes particularly helpful when recognizing that life outside of work is always in flux—sometimes gradual, sometimes all-consuming. So, how you solve things for each stage helps you imagine and create the life you want for every subsequent stage.

The result? Investing in a ThirdPath Leader mindset and developing the skills to implement the life you want are tools that will serve you for the rest of your life.

Think, for example, about these two cross-sections in time:

You as a parent	**You as an empty nester**
You: age 30-50	You: age 50-70
Your children: age 0-20	Your children: age 20-40
Your parents: 60-80	Your parents: 80-100

The needs of a family with infants and toddlers will always be very different than a family with teens. And, of course, the solutions change again as you add helping to meet the needs of your aging parents to your caregiving mix.

But it's not just about skills. The more you live a life aligned with what's important to you, the fewer regrets you will have when looking back at the choices you made.

This is where hope meets hard work. Are you ready to roll up your sleeves and make a change for the better? Are you ready to reimagine your team at home, launch an integrated career, and design a new way of doing leadership? Of course you are.

PIVOTING THROUGH WORK AND LIFE— ELIZABETH

Elizabeth has managed multiple "pivots" in her life. Most recently, this included coordinating a company-wide pivot to help her 5,000-person health care company become fully remote. Elizabeth joined this organization six years ago and is now Vice President of Employee Experience.

Elizabeth's success in pivoting to deal with the unprecedented experience of Covid was based on years of adapting to changes both in work and life and drawing from both sides of the work-life equation as she searched for new answers.

Her success also often started with a brave conversation as well. In fact, throughout her life, Elizabeth has had a number of these brave conversations.

When her son was born seventeen years ago, the world was a different place. She also had a vision of trying to be both a working person and a parent, crafting a plan that felt pretty innovative considering the lack of successful examples in her circle of friends, family, and coworkers. That's a brave thing to do.

"I would say the bravery might go back to even before my son was born. In 2000, myself and my husband at the time were both living and working in Los Angeles, but we knew we didn't want to start a family there. So, we did some research and visited a

bunch of potential cities and landed on Portland," said Elizabeth.

Although her company didn't have anyone who telecommuted, Elizabeth decided to see if they would let her work from Portland. She also knew they weren't going to fire her for asking. Elizabeth presented her boss with a proposal: "I could come down to Los Angeles every other week for four days, and the rest of the time I'd work from home in Portland." Her boss said yes.

Elizabeth imagined only commuting every other week for a short while, but the arrangement lasted for two and a half years, with the company paying for Elizabeth's travel. But once she became pregnant, it was time to pivot again.

"I decided I couldn't keep it up with a little baby. It was not going to work. It was not the kind of parent I wanted to be, you know, the one who's gone every other week. And they were also starting to look at me funny on the airlines as I got bigger and bigger. 'Lady, please don't have this baby on this plane!'"

Initially she thought she would resign after her son was born. That was until her husband was laid off. "So, there we were, with a baby and no jobs."

Fortunately, Elizabeth's former employer was happy to take her on as a part-time consultant, allowing her to work while still spending time with the new baby. This also taught Elizabeth how much "it pays to really invest in those relationships and to do good work."

Time passed, and it became clear that Elizabeth was going to be the primary income earner in the family. Elizabeth found a new job that proved to be exciting and full of opportunities for travel and success. But it also demanded a lot of time, and that took its toll.

Once again, it was time to pivot. Elizabeth wanted more time to be a parent. She also wanted time to invest in her marriage to see if she and her ex-husband could turn things around, but they couldn't.

Around this time her mother's second husband passed away. And once again, Elizabeth thoughtfully observed all of these new realities and rose to meet them.

"We sort of found ourselves meeting on a similar plane, where I was newly single and so was my mother. She was kind of thinking, what's next for me? And she had the idea of, perhaps in the future when she needed more care, moving closer to me. We started talking, and I said, 'Well, you know, if you want to spend time with your grandson, he's here now, and in four or five years, he's gone. He's off to college and doing his own thing. So if you're thinking that part of us being closer is having time with him? Well, that's kind of now.'"

After considering a number of options, her mother said, "What if we just got a big-ass house?" This

sounded appealing to Elizabeth, but life had also taught her that it would be important to test-run the idea. So that is exactly what they did.

Today, when describing how her current employer managed the changes connected to the pandemic, Elizabeth gives a lot of credit to her organization, but it's easy to see how she also drew from her own work-life experiences.

It turns out her son's school was very close to the first reported U.S. virus outbreak. When the outbreak happened, the school quickly decided to test virtual learning for a full school-day. It went so well that they continued the year fully remotely. Consequently, Elizabeth decided there was a lot to gain from doing a test-run in her organization as well.

"We told everybody to take their laptop and go home for a day." Ten days later the state instituted a stay-at-home lockdown. They were ready.

Just as before, Elizabeth had found a way to draw from both sides of her experiences—in life and work—and pivot.

"You know," Elizabeth remarked, "We're all the same people, no matter where we go, so the skills you hone at work help you be successful at home, and the skills you hone at home help you be successful at work."

She also learned, "You might not be able to solve everything at the beginning, because you don't know what is going to happen, but you can solve what is right in front of you. You can evolve." You can pivot.

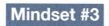
A COMMUNITY OF SUPPORT

With over two decades of work supporting parents to "Share Care" and professionals to become "ThirdPath Leaders," we've developed a wide range of tools to help people succeed at work while also creating plenty of time for their families and other life interests.

As wonderful as the tools are and as important as our research and advocacy work has been, our biggest asset is something much bigger. It's the community of people we've been developing—people who have already explored an integrated approach to work and life—each one helping us expand our learning, each one eager to share what they've learned.

Today we've have a variety of ways you can connect with this amazing community, whether it's through our biennial Pioneering Leader Summit or our introductory Overwhelm Mitigation Groups—"OMG" for short.

We hope you see our ThirdPath Leader Guide as an open invitation to get to know this amazing community. We also hope it's taught you that your commitment to both your work and life goals won't just benefit you: it will create a new way of thinking for everyone around you.

If you are ready to start on your own unique third path, take a look at the next page. We've organized our list of exercises to help you chart your new course.

Our Mission: ThirdPath Institute assists individuals, families and organizations in redesigning work and life to create time for family, community and other life priorities. We provide a road map for individuals and leaders to design an integrated approach so everyone can succeed at work while caring well for our loved ones and communities. Through this work, and in collaboration with others, we encourage more progressive conversations at home, support more flexible workplaces and push for improved public policy.

ThirdPath Institute is a 501(c)3 nonprofit organization that relies on the support of individuals in order to keep cost of services low, quality of programs high and breadth of reach expanding.

Please consider a donation!
thirdpath.org